Cool Careers in Science

- Solving crimes using science
- More than 15 career paths
- Key skills for success

FORENSIC Scientists

ALTERNATIVE REALITY DEVELOPERS

ARTIFICIAL INTELLIGENCE SCIENTISTS

COMPUTER GAME & APP DEVELOPERS

DRIVERLESS VEHICLE DEVELOPERS

DRONE PILOTS

ENTERTAINMENT ENGINEERS

FORENSIC SCIENTISTS

PROFESSIONAL HACKERS

RENEWABLE ENERGY WORKERS

ROBOTICS DEVELOPERS

Cool Careers in Science

FORENSIC Scientists

ANDREW MORKES

MASON CREST
PHILADELPHIA
MIAMI

Mason Crest
450 Parkway Drive, Suite D
Broomall, Pennsylvania 19008
(866) MCP-BOOK (toll-free)

First printing

9 8 7 6 5 4 3 2 1

HARDBACK ISBN: 978-1-4222-4299-5
SERIES ISBN: 978-1-4222-4292-6
E-BOOK ISBN: 978-1-4222-7516-0

Cataloging-in-Publication Data on file with the Library of Congress

Developed and Produced by National Highlights, Inc.
Interior and cover design: Jana Rade, impact studios
Interior layout: Annalisa Gumbrecht, Studio Gumbrecht
Production: Michelle Luke
Proofreader: Susan Uttendorfsky

QR CODES AND LINKS TO THIRD-PARTY CONTENT

Table of Contents

KEY ICONS TO LOOK FOR:

WORDS TO UNDERSTAND: These words with their easy-to-understand definitions will increase the reader's understanding of the text while building vocabulary skills.

SIDEBARS: This boxed material within the main text allows readers to build knowledge, gain insights, explore possibilities, and broaden their perspectives by weaving together additional information to provide realistic and holistic perspectives.

EDUCATIONAL VIDEOS: Readers can view videos by scanning our QR codes, providing them with additional educational content to supplement the text. Examples include news coverage, moments in history, speeches, iconic sports moments, and much more!

TEXT-DEPENDENT QUESTIONS: These questions send the reader back to the text for more careful attention to the evidence presented there.

RESEARCH PROJECTS: Readers are pointed toward areas of further inquiry connected to each chapter. Suggestions are provided for projects that encourage deeper research and analysis.

Introduction

CAREERS IN SCIENCE OFFER GOOD PAY, THE OPPORTUNITY TO HELP PEOPLE, AND OTHER REWARDS

Where would we be without science? Well, we'd be without computers, smartphones, and other cutting-edge technologies. Crimes would take longer to solve without modern forensic analysis techniques. More of our private information would be stolen by hackers. We'd be stuck relying on environmentally harmful fossil fuels instead of using renewable energy. And life would be less fun because we wouldn't have drones, awe-inspiring and physics-defying roller coasters, and the computer and video games that we play for hours.

Job markets are sometimes strong and sometimes weak, but a career in science (which, for the purposes of this series, includes the related fields of technology and engineering) is almost a sure path to a comfortable life. The following paragraphs provide more information on why a career in science is a great choice.

Good pay. People in science careers earn some of the highest salaries in the work world. The median annual (yearly) salary for those in life, physical, and social science careers in the United States is $64,510, according to the U.S. Department of Labor (USDL). This is much higher than the median earnings ($37,690) for all careers. Additionally, the median salary for those in computer and mathematical occupations is $84,575, and for engineers, it's

$79,180. Science professionals who become managers or who launch their own businesses can earn anywhere from $150,000 to $300,000 or more a year.

Strong employment prospects. There are shortages of science workers throughout the world according to the consulting firm ManpowerGroup. In fact, engineering workers are the third most in-demand employees in the world. Technicians rank fourth, and computer and information technology professionals rank sixth.

There's a shortage of software engineers in more than twenty countries, including the United States, Canada, Mexico, Japan, and the United Kingdom, according to the recruitment firm Michael Page. Other science careers where there is a shortage of workers include electronics engineers (nineteen countries), electrical engineers (sixteen countries), data analysts (eleven countries), and hardware engineers (six countries), among others.

The USDL predicts that employment of computer and information technology professionals in the United States will grow by 13 percent during the next decade. Career opportunities for those in life, physical, and social science occupations will grow by 10 percent. Both of these career fields are growing faster than the average for all careers. The outlook is also good for engineering professionals. Employment is expected to grow by 7 percent during the next decade. The strongest opportunities will be found in renewable energy and robotics.

By 2026, the USDL predicts that there will be more than 876,000 new jobs in the science, technology, engineering, and mathematics fields.

Rewarding work environment and many career options. A career in science is fulfilling because you get to use both your creative and practical sides to develop new technologies (or improve existing ones), solve problems, and make the world a better place. There's a common misconception that science workers spend most of their time in dreary, windowless laboratories. While they do spend lots of time in the laboratory, they also spend time in the field testing, troubleshooting, and trying out their inventions or discoveries. Forensic scientists, the subject of this book, spend much of their time at crime scenes and accident sites. Some science professionals launch their own businesses, which can be both fun and very rewarding.

Job opportunities are available throughout the United States and the world. Science professionals play such an important role in our modern world that there are jobs almost anywhere, although many positions are found in urban areas.

IS A CAREER IN SCIENCE RIGHT FOR ME?

Test your interest. How many of these statements do you agree with?

___ I like to learn about scientific breakthroughs.

___ I like to use technology to solve problems.

___ I enjoy doing science experiments.

___ I enjoy coming up with ideas on how to solve the world's problems.

___ I am curious about how things work.

___ I like to invent things.

___ I am creative and have a good imagination.

___ I enjoy computer science classes.

___ I like to build electronics and other things that require electricity.

___ I am good at math.

If many of the statements above describe you, then you should consider a career in the sciences. But you don't need to select a career right now. Check out this book on a career as a forensic scientist—as well as other books in the series—to learn more about occupational paths in the sciences and related fields. Good luck with your career exploration!

WORDS TO UNDERSTAND

civil case: a type of legal situation in which a person or entity (such as a company or the government), called the plaintiff, claims that another entity or person (the defendant) has failed to perform a legal duty promised to the plaintiff

civilian: a person who is not a member of the police or the military

DNA profiling: the process of identifying genetic markers to uniquely identify a person; a person's DNA profile is as unique as their fingerprints

testify: to provide evidence as a witness in a court of law

Chapter 1

WHAT DO FORENSIC SCIENTISTS DO?

THE WORLD OF FORENSIC SCIENCE

If the terms **DNA profiling**, blood splatter, and rigor mortis fascinate you rather than gross you out, then a career as a forensic scientist solving crimes might be in your future. But forensic science is a lot more than just crime scene investigation. Forensic scientists work in many other areas, including fire investigation, computer crime, anthropology, engineering, and nursing. Although there are many forensic science specialties, a few things are certain: Careers in forensic science are exciting, rewarding, and well paying.

WHAT IS FORENSIC SCIENCE?

To understand the meaning of the phrase forensic science, let's define both words. The term forensic comes from the Latin (an ancient language) word *forensis*, which means "for public discussion or debate." A modern definition of the word forensic translates into "for use in a court of law." We all know what science is, so the meaning of forensic science is "scientific findings that are used in a court of law."

The use of mobile crime investigation laboratories has increased the speed at which evidence can be collected and analyzed.

Forensic science is used in courtrooms, but not every forensic scientist goes to court to **testify**. Many never do so. They use forensic science to settle **civil cases**, help governments gather information, enforce laws, protect the public, and help a company or other organization determine the facts about an event, substance, or product. Others use forensic science to find out what caused a fire or a bridge collapse.

KEY DUTIES FOR FORENSIC SCIENTISTS

There are many types of forensic scientists. Although their work responsibilities vary by specialty, most forensic scientists perform the following tasks:

- Collect physical evidence at crime scenes
- Take photographs and videos and sketch diagrams at crime scenes

Learn more about educational requirements, key skills for success, and careers in forensic science

- Use various tools and instruments, such as microscopes, to study evidence in laboratories
- Write reports that summarize their findings
- Testify, often as expert witnesses, during legal proceedings about their research and conclusions; expert witnesses have expertise in a particular field (such as engineering or pathology), and are qualified to give opinion testimony in court, which a nonexpert witness may be prohibited from providing

DID YOU KNOW?

The American Academy of Forensic Sciences reports that more than 100,000 photographs and 13,000 digital videos were reviewed to catch the terrorists who committed the Boston Marathon bombing in 2013.

CAREER PATHS IN FORENSIC SCIENCE

There are many career paths in forensic science. The following sections provide more information on specialties.

COMPUTER AND DIGITAL FORENSICS

Cybercrime is a major problem in the United States and throughout the world. CNBC.com reports that "cyber theft is the fastest-growing crime in the U.S., and cost the global economy more than $450 billion in 2016, with more than 2 billion personal records stolen." Additionally, computers, mobile phones, the internet, and other types of technology are used by criminals in the act of committing a murder or assault, robbing a gas station or department store, or committing many other crimes. As a result, demand for *computer and digital forensics scientists and investigators* is strong. These professionals conduct digital forensic examinations of computers, tablets, smartphones, photographs, video and digital audio recordings, smart home technology (devices that are connected to the internet and other devices that share information), and other types of technology. To learn more, visit the following websites:

- High Technology Crime Investigation Association, www.htcia.org
- International Association of Computer Investigative Specialists, www.iacis.com

DID YOU KNOW?

U.S. News & World Report recently ranked the career of forensic science technician as one of the top ten science careers.

CRIME SCENE INVESTIGATION

Crime scene investigators (CSIs) collect evidence at the scenes of violent crimes, burglaries, fires, auto thefts and accidents, suicides, and other incidents or accidents. They have different titles depending on where they

A forensic science technician photographs a bloodstained knife at a crime scene.

work and their job duties. They may be called *criminalists, forensic science technicians, crime scene technicians, forensic investigators, crime scene analysts, evidence technicians,* and *criminalistics officers*. In the past, most CSIs were police officers who had completed some training in forensic investigation. While specially trained police officers still work as CSIs, many departments are hiring **civilian** workers who have bachelor's degrees in a natural science, such as chemistry or biology, or in forensic science. CSIs work at crime scenes and laboratories and may appear in court.

CRIME SCENES

CSIs have many duties at crime scenes. They secure the area to protect evidence from being disturbed or tampered with and determine what evidence, such as fingerprints, bodily fluids, weapons, and bullet casings, should be collected and how. They are also often tasked with taking photographs and videos of the crime scene and evidence, as well as castings of footprints, tire marks, and tool mark impressions. They may make sketches of the crime scene and often take notes about the location and position of evidence, weather conditions, and other details. All of this is useful as they reconstruct a crime scene.

LABORATORIES

In laboratories, CSIs conduct biological, chemical, genetic, and microscopic analyses on evidence collected from crime scenes. They also consult with and follow instructions from forensic chemists, toxicologists, biologists, and other scientists. They often write reports about their findings.

COURTROOMS

CSIs are often called upon to testify about their findings in legal and civil proceedings. As a result, they need excellent communication skills.

FURTHER RESOURCES

For more information on education and careers in crime scene investigation, visit these sites:

- Association for Crime Scene Reconstruction, www.acsr.org
- International Association of Bloodstain Pattern Analysts, www.iabpa.org
- International Crime Scene Investigators Association, www.icsia.org

A DAY IN THE LIFE: CRIME SCENE INVESTIGATOR

I've worked as a crime scene investigator for a police department on the West Coast of the United States for nearly ten years. I love my job because I enjoy solving riddles (I love crosswords, too!) and playing a role in fighting crime.

On a typical day, we receive calls to collect evidence at a variety of scenes—from a car or home break-in to the site of a sexual assault to a murder scene. Today, my first assignment is at the site of an attempted car theft. When I get to the site, I begin by using a brush and powder to dust the exterior of the car for fingerprints. Once I identify fingerprints, I photograph them and use adhesive tape to lift them from the window. These will be compared against those in fingerprint databases to identify suspects.

I identify and collect other types of evidence such as tool marks, footprints, and tire prints. I photograph the impression and, in some cases, make a cast of it. To do so, I fill the impression with a compound that hardens and keeps the shape and characteristics of the impression.

Some items can't be tested on site. In this instance, I collect the items and place them in tamper-resistant evidence bags so that they can be analyzed at the laboratory.

I do a lot of bending, stooping, and crawling at crime scenes. I might have to crawl underneath a car to photograph and collect a piece of evidence, or climb a steep hill to get to a murder site. I love this job, but it can be repetitious at times. Not every crime is worthy of a *CSI*-level focus. In this career, you spend a lot of time doing tasks (such as dusting for fingerprints, collecting blood and hair samples, and collecting bullet casings) over and over. It takes a detail-oriented person with a deliberate and calm personality to be successful as a crime scene investigator. You also need to be a good communicator and team player because you'll be working with other CSIs, police officers, and forensic scientists. Writing skills are very important because your reports must pass the scrutiny of the defendant's lawyer in court. If your report is full of errors or is confusing in some way, it will be picked apart by the defendant's lawyer and the case could be thrown out by the judge. Despite the sometimes challenging nature of this job, I wouldn't trade my career for anything.

FINGERPRINT ANALYSIS

Fingerprints have been collected and analyzed to solve crimes for more than 150 years. They can be found on almost any solid surface—even the human body. Fingerprints are classifieds into three categories.

PLASTIC PRINTS

Plastic prints are those that are often three-dimensional and found on soft surfaces (such as soap, wax, fresh caulk, wet paint, etc.).

PATENT PRINTS

Patent prints are visible prints that are found on hard surfaces. They occur when blood, dirt, ink, paint, or another substance on a thumb or finger is transferred to surfaces that are porous (such as paper or wood) or nonporous (glass, metal, or plastic).

A fingerprint analyst studies a fingerprint that was recently recovered at the scene of an attempted home break-in.

LATENT PRINTS

Latent prints are invisible prints that are found on hard surfaces.

FINGERPRINT COLLECTION

Patent fingerprints are typically collected via high-resolution photography. A forensic measurement scale is included in the image for reference.

Latent prints are discovered by dusting a surface with fingerprint powder. Then the *fingerprint analyst* photographs the fingerprint, uses clear adhesive tape to lift the print from the surface, and places it on a latent lift card so it can be preserved as evidence.

Using fingerprint powder can damage evidence and limit the techniques that can be used to discover latent prints. As a result, fingerprint analysts are increasingly using lasers and LED devices that emit a particular wavelength, or spectrum, of light to look for fingerprints on windowsills, door handles, railings, and other surfaces at crime scenes.

Cyanoacrylate (superglue) processing, or fuming, is another technique that can be done instead of, or before, using fingerprint powder. This process, which is usually performed on nonporous surfaces such as glass, involves exposing an object (such as a door handle) to cyanoacrylate vapors (fumes). The vapors stick to any latent prints, and the prints can be detected by using a light source.

Once a fingerprint analyst obtains fingerprints from a crime scene or a piece of evidence, they compare them with those that were collected from the scenes of similar crimes. A fingerprint analyst may refer to files they maintain on recent crimes and note any similarities between them. Today, new fingerprints are added and compared to existing fingerprints in a computer database that is known as an "automated fingerprint identification system." These systems have greatly improved the speed at which new fingerprints can be matched to those that are already on file.

FIRE INVESTIGATION

Fires are a major cause of injury, death, and property destruction in the United States and around the world. *Fire investigators* conduct investigations at the scenes of fires and collect and study evidence to determine if the fire started accidentally or was deliberately set (arson). People commit arson to obtain insurance money, to cover up a crime at the site, because they are angry at the property owner or someone who lives in the building, or because they want to commit senseless vandalism (destruction of property).

In the past, most fire investigations were conducted by firefighters or others who did not have training in the forensic sciences. But today, many fire investigators have degrees in fire science or a forensic science specialty (such as chemistry).

Fire investigators travel to fire scenes—ideally while the fire is still burning—to gather evidence, observe the properties of the fire (if it is still burning), and

Fire investigators in Hong Kong review evidence collected after a suspicious fire destroyed several shops.

interview witnesses. Later, they review photos and video of the scene that were taken before, during, and after the fire. They write reports about their findings and testify in court. They work with police to identify arson suspects. Fire investigators may also prepare damage estimates for reporting and insurance purposes.

Visit the websites of the following organizations for more information on education and careers in fire investigation:

- International Association of Arson Investigators, www.firearson.com
- International Association of Bomb Technicians and Investigators, www.iabti.org
- National Association of Fire Investigators, www.nafi.org

MYTHS AND FACTS ABOUT FORENSIC SCIENCE

Television crime shows are fun to watch, but they don't always get the facts right. Here are some myths about forensic science work that are often presented on TV and the realities.

Myth: Crime scenes are processed quickly, and lab results are provided to police in under twenty-four hours.

Fact: Collecting and processing takes days and even weeks depending on the number of laboratory staff. For a typical case, DNA processing and analysis can take more than fifty hours.

Myth: Every police department and crime lab has expensive equipment that helps solve crimes quickly.

Fact: Most organizations do not have the budgets to have cutting-edge technology on hand.

Myth: Every day on the job is exciting and filled with action.

Fact: Work as a forensic scientist and technician can be boring and repetitious. They often have to perform the same tests over and over. Writing detailed reports can be time consuming and boring, but it's extremely important that reports are prepared properly so that they can be used in court.

Myth: Crime scene work and investigative work is done by the same people.

Fact: These are two separate functions. The crime scene technician collects evidence, but they rarely participate in investigations with the police.

FORENSIC ANTHROPOLOGY

Physical anthropologists study the biology and evolution of humans and closely related primates (apes, monkeys, etc.) and how it has changed over the years. *Forensic anthropologists* are specialized physical anthropologists who study human remains. They work at the site of a car, plane, or train crash; at a suspected crime scene; at the scene of a battle that was fought recently or decades ago; in laboratories; and at other locations. The first step that they take is to determine if the remains are human or animal or a mix of the two. Human and animal bones can become intermingled. If the bones are identified as human, the forensic anthropologist creates a biological profile of the deceased individual, which estimates the person's age (by studying their bones and teeth), sex, height, and, in some cases, ancestry (one's family or ethnic descent). The biological profile helps the forensic anthropologist and law enforcement authorities narrow the pool of people who are missing in a particular area. More specific tests (X-rays, DNA analysis, dental record analysis) are conducted to compare the individual's characteristics to that of a small number of missing persons who have the same characteristics (e.g., male, aged twenty to thirty, Asian descent). The forensic anthropologist then uses these and other tests to match the individual with a missing person. They then try to determine the cause of death of the individual.

Sometimes, forensic anthropologists don't even start out with a body to study. Law enforcement officials may ask forensic anthropologists to use their knowledge of crime scenes and the environment to look for a body or a mass grave in a certain area. Once they find the body or bodies, the forensic anthropologist uses modified archaeological techniques to recover the remains and any other evidence. Then they study the remains to create a biological profile and try to identify the person or persons.

Forensic anthropologists work in other settings. If an old cemetery is in the path of a new highway, for example, they help remove and relocate bodies so that the project can be completed. Others work in museums to catalog and curate ancient human remains. Still others specialize in facial reconstruction, which is the art of attempting to re-create the appearance of an unidentified person's face from the features of their skull.

To learn more about forensic anthropology, visit these sites:

- American Anthropological Association, www.americananthro.org
- American Board of Forensic Anthropology, www.theabfa.org

FORENSIC BALLISTICS

Some forensic scientists specialize in firearms investigation and ballistics. CrimeMuseum.org defines ballistics as the "study of motion, dynamics, angular movement, and effects of projectile units (bullets, missiles, and bombs)." Forensic ballistics and firearms investigators often study guns and the bullets that they fire. Microscopic marks are made on the surfaces of bullets and cartridge cases every time a gun is fired. When a crime occurs, scientists study these marks to link bullets and cartridge cases to suspected criminals. They often testify in legal proceedings about their findings. They first explain how firearms and ammunition work to juries, judges, and lawyers. Then they answer certain questions:

- What kind of firearm was used in the alleged crime?
- What kind of ammunition was used?
- What position was the bullet fired from? (This helps law enforcement officials determine if a shooting was an accident, self-defense, suicide, or a homicide.)

To learn more, visit the Association of Firearm and Tool Mark Examiners website, https://afte.org/about-us/what-is-afte/what-is-firearm-and-tool-mark-identification.

FORENSIC SCIENTIST CAREER PATH

Within a few years of hard work, you can advance to managerial positions or even start your own consulting business. Here's a typical career ladder for forensic scientists:

Forensic Science Consultant

Forensic Science Laboratory Manager

Forensic Scientist

Scientist

Forensic Science Technician or Intern

FORENSIC BOTANY

Botanists conduct scientific study of plants, which can be broadly defined as including algae, fungi, lichens, mosses, ferns, conifers, and flowering plants. *Forensic botanists* use scientific principles and their knowledge of genetics to collect and analyze plants that are found at crime scenes, or in or on the bodies of crime victims or those who have died under mysterious circumstances. This plant evidence can range from large pieces of wood or twigs to leaves to other parts of the plant that are visible to the naked eye. Forensic botanists also collect and study microscopic samples of seeds, spores, and pollen. Their analysis provides information that can link a suspect to a crime (if unique plant evidence is found on their clothing, for example), determine if a person was killed at the crime scene or if their body was moved there from another location, and determine the time of year at which the murder or other event took place. The Botanical Society of America is a good source for more information about forensic botany (www.botany.org).

FORENSIC CHEMISTRY

Chemists study substances at the atomic and molecular levels. *Forensic chemists* are specialized chemists who analyze physical evidence and samples to help

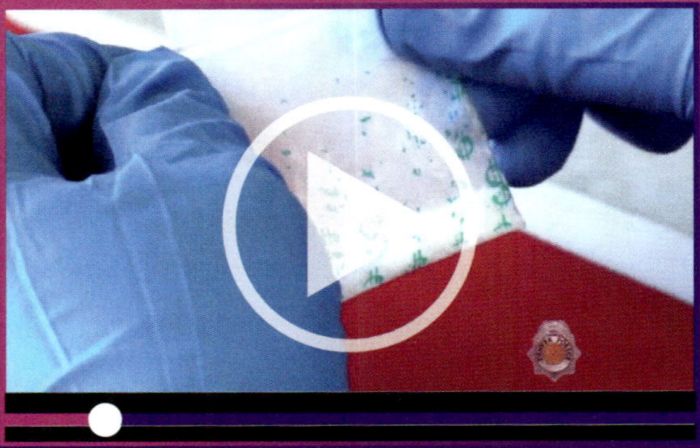

Learn more about the Forensic Chemistry Unit at the Denver Police Crime Lab

solve crimes. They seek to identify unknown materials and match samples to known substances. They also analyze drugs and controlled substances taken from scenes and people. Controlled substances are drugs and chemicals whose production, possession, or use are regulated by a government. These substances often have a negative effect on a person's health and welfare.

FORENSIC DENTISTRY

Dentists diagnose and treat problems with our teeth, gums, and related parts of the mouth. *Forensic dentists* are forensic scientists who use their dental knowledge to identify human remains, conduct bite mark analyses, analyze dental injuries and neglect in cases of abuse, and resolve dental malpractice or negligence issues (when a dentist doesn't perform their job correctly). They are also known as *forensic odontologists*.

Forensic dentists spend much of their workday identifying human remains. In many cases—such as when bodies have been severely damaged by fires, natural disasters, explosions, or other events that have caused advanced decomposition—a single tooth or a fragment of a jaw may be the only parts of the body that can be used to identify an individual (if pre-death dental X-rays are available for comparison). For death investigations, forensic odontologists attend autopsies and gather information by taking photographs, taking dental measurements, making dental impressions (an imprint of the teeth and mouth), and reviewing copies of X-rays. They also visit crime scenes and places where accidents and natural disasters have occurred to gather evidence.

Forensic odontologists also conduct bite mark analyses and other investigations to identify perpetrators who committed rape, domestic violence, assault, elder abuse, or other crimes.

Contact the American Society of Forensic Odontology (www.asfo.org) to learn more about forensic dentistry.

A chemist uses gas chromatography to test food for suspected contamination.

FORENSIC DOCUMENT EXAMINATION

Forensic document examination, which is also known as "questioned document examination," involves the authentication (the process of verifying if something is real or true) of signatures and handwriting, but also the analysis of writing instruments, writing mediums, and office machine products. The goal of these analyses is to determine authenticity and other facts for legal and civil proceedings. According to the American Society of Forensic Sciences, *forensic document examiners* perform the following tasks:

- Verification of authorship of signatures, handwriting, and hand printing
- Examination of documents for evidence of alterations (changes)
- Decipherment of destroyed or erased entries
- Restoration of liquid-soaked or burned documents
- Classification and identification of typewriters, printers, and other office products such as staplers or check writers

- Verification of page substitution in documents
- Examination of the presence of indented writings (impression made on a second page of a document by writing on the first page)

The types of documents that are examined include wills, deeds, income tax records, contracts, time sheets, medical records, loan agreements, election petitions, checks, autographed memorabilia, and anonymous letters.

You can learn more about this field by visiting the websites of the following organizations:

- American Board of Forensic Document Examiners, www.abfde.org
- American Society of Questioned Document Examiners, www.asqde.org

FORENSIC ENGINEERING

Engineers use scientific, engineering, and mathematics principles to design, troubleshoot, and improve everything from smartphones to bridges and jet fighters. *Forensic engineers* conduct investigations to determine what caused the malfunction or complete failure of airplanes, bridges, products, and other objects and structures. The cause may be mechanical or chemical breakdown or failure, or a criminal act. Forensic engineers study mechanisms, fluids (gases and liquids), heat, sound, electricity, and any other system, energy source, or subject that may cause something to malfunction or fail. They also investigate the causes of environmental disasters or accidents. Forensic engineers provide reports that are used as evidence in criminal cases, contract or warranty disputes, personal-injury lawsuits, and patent and copyright infringement litigation. To learn more about forensic engineering, contact these organizations:

- National Academy of Forensic Engineers, www.nafe.org
- Society of Forensic Engineers and Scientists, www.sfes.us

DID YOU KNOW?

Forensic engineers conducted engineering studies to determine why both towers of the World Trade Center in New York City collapsed so quickly after the terrorist attacks on September 11, 2001. Experts still disagree on what caused the quick collapse of the towers, but many cite the force of the initial impact of the two planes, which caused significant damage to the buildings' external and core columns, and a weakening of the steel superstructure caused by fire that was fueled by massive amounts of jet fuel.

FORENSIC ENTOMOLOGY

Entomologists are scientists who study insects. They are experts on where insects live, their life cycle (birth to death), and their behaviors. *Forensic entomologists* conduct scientific studies of insect evidence for use in legal or civil proceedings. There are three main types of forensic entomology: medicolegal forensic entomology, stored-product forensic entomology, and urban forensic entomology.

MEDICOLEGAL FORENSIC ENTOMOLOGY

Medicolegal forensic entomology is the best-known specialty. These specialists travel to crime scenes or places where an unexplained death has occurred to study and record the conditions at the scene and collect insect evidence (insects, eggs, etc.) from the crime scene, the area around the body, and on the external area of the body. They also study insects and eggs that have been removed by forensic pathologists from inside a body. They do so to determine when trauma occurred (before or after death), identify the individual (from DNA collected), record toxicological results (the effects of chemicals on the body), determine if the remains were moved from one location to another, and answer many other questions.

Forensic entomologists can study the presence and growth stages of maggots on corpses to estimate the time of death.

STORED-PRODUCT FORENSIC ENTOMOLOGY

Stored-product forensic entomologists work with bug infestations (a large number of unwanted insects) in stored products, often food. They use their knowledge of insects' reproductive habits, growth cycles, feeding behavior, typical habitat (where they live), physical characteristics, and other criteria to determine when and how an infestation began. They may discover that an infestation occurred during the packaging process, or that it occurred at a warehouse where the product was being stored before sale.

URBAN FORENSIC ENTOMOLOGY

Urban forensic entomologists study insect infestations—often cockroaches and bedbugs—in homes, businesses, schools, hotels, hospitals, and other buildings. They identify the species, the level of infestation, and how the infestation occurred and how it can be stopped.

For more information about forensic entomology, contact these organizations:

- American Board of Forensic Entomology, www.forensicentomologist.org
- The Entomological Society of America, www.entsoc.org
- North American Forensic Entomology Association, www.nafea.net

FORENSIC NURSING

We all know that *nurses* care for the sick and injured. But did you know that there are nurses who work in the field of forensic science? *Forensic nurses* care for victims of violent or abusive acts, then collect evidence that can be used in a court of law to catch and prosecute those who have committed these acts. They work in many specialties, including sexual assault, child abuse and neglect, elder abuse, domestic violence, death investigations, and the aftermath of mass murders. In addition to their medical skills, forensic nurses have completed specialized training in identifying, evaluating, and documenting injuries. They also are knowledgeable about the legal system so that they can prepare legal reports, testify in court, and interact with legal professionals, judges, and juries. The International Association of Forensic Nurses (www.forensicnurses.org) provides more information on education and careers in the field.

FORENSIC PATHOLOGY

Pathologists, who are also known as *medical examiners*, study the bodies of people who have died—most often, those who have died unexpectedly or violently. *Forensic pathologists* use the principles of pathology and medicine to obtain facts that can be used in legal and civil proceedings. They are best known for performing autopsies, but they also study the decedent's medical history, visit crimes scenes to gather evidence, review witness statements, and collect medical and trace evidence from the exterior of the body (including the decedent's clothes and personal effects) to determine the cause of death. The cause may be murder, natural causes, suicide, accidental, or unknown.

Most people associate forensic pathologists with murder cases, but they also investigate sudden deaths of healthy people, suspicious or unusual deaths, deaths that occur in police custody, and some deaths that occur in prisons.

Clinical forensic pathologists examine living patients who have been sexually assaulted or abused in other ways.

Contact the American Society for Investigative Pathology (www.asip.org) to learn more about this career.

FORENSIC TOXICOLOGY

Toxicologists study the adverse (negative) effects of chemicals on living organisms. Forensic toxicologists use toxicology in a medicolegal context—meaning that their medical findings are used in courts of law and civil proceedings. There are several forensic toxicology specialties.

POSTMORTEM FORENSIC TOXICOLOGY

Postmortem forensic toxicologists work to establish the role of alcohol, illegal and prescription drugs, poisons, metals, and other types of chemicals and substances in the manner and cause of deaths. They work in laboratories to study a wide variety of specimens provided by forensic pathologists and other forensic science professionals. Specimens include blood, hair and nails, urine, and vitreous (clear) fluid from the brain, eye, liver, and other tissues.

HUMAN PERFORMANCE FORENSIC TOXICOLOGY

Human performance forensic toxicologists study the effects of alcohol and drugs on human behavior and performance. They typically collect samples (which can include body fluids, hair, and other substances) from living persons. The goal of this work is to provide information to law enforcement officials who are conducting investigations into impaired driving, sexual assaults, vehicular assault and homicide, and other incidents where alcohol and drugs may be involved.

FORENSIC DRUG-TESTING

Forensic drug-testing scientists conduct tests on workers in almost any field, but especially those in safety-sensitive fields such as law enforcement, transportation, and the military. They also conduct tests on college, Olympic, and professional athletes, and those who have been convicted of a crime and have been put on probation or paroled from prison.

Visit the following websites to learn more about education and careers in forensic toxicology:

- International Association of Forensic Toxicologists, www.tiaft.org
- Society of Forensic Toxicologists, Inc., www.soft-tox.org
- Society of Toxicology, www.toxicology.org

A forensic toxicologist uses a mass spectrometer to conduct a test.

OTHER FORENSIC SCIENCE SPECIALTIES

There are many other specialties in forensic science.

Forensic meteorologists help reconstruct weather events for a certain time and location.

Forensic psychiatrists and *psychologists* testify in court regarding the mental state of defendants, confirm or dispute the testimony of other mental health professionals, explain psychiatric/psychological concepts to juries and judges, and advise lawyers and other legal professionals about psychiatric/psychological issues that might have an effect on legal proceedings.

Forensic microbiologists study bacteria, archaea, and microbial eukaryotes to determine the cause of death, manner of death, identification, and postmortem interval (the time since death).

Forensic veterinarians examine animals to detect and document trauma.

Forensic accountants and auditors use accounting, auditing, and forensic science principles to support or oppose claims being made during legal or civil proceedings.

WORK ENVIRONMENTS

Work environments for forensic scientists vary by specialty and employer.

LABORATORIES AND RESEARCH FACILITIES

Many forensic scientists work in comfortable, climate-controlled laboratories and research facilities. They may also have a cubicle or small office where they write reports, do other paperwork, conduct research in databases and on the internet, and meet with members of their team.

COLLEGES

Many forensic scientists work as college professors in their main job and provide consulting services to law enforcement agencies and other employers on an as-needed basis. When they are on call, their workday can last as long as ten to twelve hours. A typical day might involve teaching classes during the day and then being called to the scene of a crime at 10 p.m., when others are heading for bed. Other forensic scientists work for crime laboratories, law enforcement agencies, and human rights organizations. They may have a more traditional nine-to-five schedule, although night and weekend work may be occasionally required.

IN THE FIELD

Forensic science professionals work at a wide range of crime or accident scenes, including cramped basements, fields, ponds, mountains, and the sites of airplane and train crashes, to name a few.

THE CHALLENGES OF BEING A FORENSIC SCIENTIST

Although forensic science can be exciting, fascinating, and rewarding, it also has some serious drawbacks. It's important to understand the pros and cons of a career in forensic science before you enter the field. Classes, internships, and part-time jobs are a good way to learn more about the field before you enter it.

The most important potential con is that, for many forensic science positions, you will work with human (and sometimes animal) remains that are in various states of decomposition. As a result, this career can be messy, smelly, and disturbing. Interns and new forensic science professionals may feel faint the first time they see a dead body. There's nothing wrong with feeling shocked or bothered at the initial sight/smell of human remains. But this is part of the job, and you will either get used to it or have to find another career.

In addition to human remains, you will need to become comfortable occasionally working around maggots and other bugs that may colonize (live on) on a corpse. This can be disturbing, but if you plan to work in forensic science, you will need to get used to working around insects.

Crimes scenes can be challenging at times. Outdoor sites can be muddy, wet, slippery, or steep. Scientists and technicians work outside in all types of weather conditions. It can be challenging to collect and preserve evidence during a rainstorm, in extreme cold or heat, or during a blizzard.

It can be emotionally exhausting to be a forensic scientist or technician. You'll be working at crime scenes where murders were committed, or be assigned to help identify dozens of corpses at the scene of an airplane crash. The facts of a case—especially those that involve children—can be very disturbing and sad.

Forensic scientists work in a variety of environments, including laboratories.

Finally, forensic scientists frequently handle and test bodily fluids such as blood and urine. These fluids can contain dangerous bacteria or diseases such as HIV/AIDS and hepatitis B and C. Scientists and technicians also may be exposed to hazardous chemicals when recovering bodies from house or car fires, explosions, etc. To protect themselves from harmful biological and chemical agents, scientists and technicians wear protective gloves, face shields, respirators, and other safety equipment.

Don't be turned off by the potential negatives of work in forensic science. Every forensic scientist and technician had to get used to seeing and smelling human remains for the first time. Every scientist had to get used to the sad stories and disturbing crime scenes. And every scientist and technician had to get used to the environmental, biological, chemical, and physical challenges of working at a crime scene or accident site.

FORENSIC SCIENCE OFFERS MANY REWARDS

Most people who become forensic scientists and technicians stay in the field because the work is interesting, challenging (in a good way), and fulfilling, and they enjoy solving problems and using science to fight crimes or solve mysteries. Additionally, the pay is good and the demand is strong for skilled workers.

TEXT-DEPENDENT QUESTIONS:

1. What is forensic science?
2. What is the difference between a forensic biologist and a forensic archaeologist?
3. What are questioned documents?

RESEARCH PROJECT:

What were the three most interesting forensic science specialties in this chapter? Conduct research to learn more about each specialty, write a report that provides more information on each field, and present this information to your science class.

MIDDLE

Chapter 2

TERMS OF THE TRADE

3-D scanner: Technology that is either used at a crime scene or another investigation site to create a large overview map of a scene, or to capture individual objects in high resolution and full color.

accelerant: Any substance that can enhance the speed of a natural or chemical reaction; gasoline, diesel fuel, kerosene, turpentine, and butane are examples of accelerants.

accident reconstruction: The process of using physical evidence to re-create an accident scene to determine what happened.

arch: A type of friction ridge pattern that appears on the pads of the fingers and thumbs, as well as on the palms, toes, and feet. This wave-like pattern makes up about 5 percent of all pattern types.

arson: Deliberately starting a fire.

autopsy: A scientific process in which a decedent's body is dissected (cut into) and the organs and other components are analyzed to determine what caused their death, or to obtain other information.

ballistics: The scientific study of firearms and projectiles.

barefoot morphology: The science of assessing and studying footprints at a crime scene in order to determine the pace, size, and body weight of a person.

biological profile: A collection of educated guesses that a forensic anthropologist makes about an unidentified person's age (by studying their bones and teeth), sex, height, and ancestry (in some cases) after examining a skeleton or other human remains.

blood spatter: The manner in which blood falls from a body or animal and impacts surfaces.

blood spatter pattern analysis: The study of blood spatter patterns to determine what took place before, during, and after the spilling of the blood.

bullet track: The path a projectile takes as it passes through a person, object, or other type of matter.

cause of death: A disease or injury that ultimately leads to the death of an individual; cause of death is sometimes determined by an autopsy.

chain of custody: The method of proving that a piece of evidence is the actual piece of evidence that was recovered at the crime scene. The chain of custody must be well documented and detail that a piece of evidence has been in the possession of forensic science and law professionals from the time of collection to its introduction in court.

chain of evidence: A series of steps (identification and collection, analysis, storage, preservation, transportation, and presentation in court) that must be followed and documented when collecting evidence and introducing it in a legal proceeding.

chromatograph: Laboratory technology that is used to separate mixed substances into their separate components in order to identify them correctly, or link evidence to a suspect.

civil case: A type of legal situation in which a person or entity (such as a company or the government), called the plaintiff, claims that another entity or person (the defendant) has failed to perform a legal duty promised to the plaintiff.

cold case: An unsolved crime that is still open but that is no longer being actively investigated by a law enforcement agency.

computer and digital forensics: The examination of computers, smartphones, smart home technology, photos, videos, audio, and other technology for evidence of innocence or wrongdoing.

controlled substance: A drug or chemical whose production, possession, or use is regulated by a government; these substances often have a negative effect on a person's health and welfare.

corpse: A dead body; also known as a cadaver.

crime scene investigation: The process of securing a crime scene, collecting physical evidence, taking photographs and videos, and otherwise creating a record of the scene for further analysis.

crime scene reconstruction: The process of using physical evidence to re-create a crime scene to find out what happened.

crime scene staging: The process of changing a crime scene (i.e., removing or moving evidence, introducing objects that were not part of the original crime, etc.) in order to confuse investigators.

criminalistics: The use of chemistry, molecular biology, geology, and other scientific disciplines to investigate and solve crimes.

CSI effect: A belief held by some law enforcement professionals and prosecutors that forensic science television dramas have negatively influenced jurors to expect more forensic evidence to convict criminal defendants.

decedent: A dead person.

decompose: Decaying or breaking down; this term is often used to describe what happens to the human body after a person dies.

DNA: Deoxyribonucleic acid; the genetic material that is found in cells.

DNA profiling: The process of identifying genetic markers to uniquely identify a person; a person's DNA profile is as unique as their fingerprints.

dusting: One of the most common methods of detecting and collecting latent fingerprints. In this process, investigators use fingerprint powder (black granular, aluminum flake, black magnetic, etc.) to dust an area, and detected prints are photographed, then lifted from the surface with clear adhesive tape.

evidence: Facts and other information that are gathered to support or disprove a belief.

expert witness: A person testifying in court who has expertise in a particular field (such as engineering or pathology) and who is entitled to give opinion testimony that a nonexpert witness may be prohibited from giving.

facial reconstruction: The art of attempting to re-create the appearance of an unidentified person's face from the features of their skull.

fingerprint: Unique patterns that appear on the pads of the fingers and thumbs.

fingerprint analysis: The study and matching of fingerprints collected at a crime scene with those collected from recent similar crimes, or those archived in automated fingerprint identification systems.

fire investigation: An investigation at the scene of a fire that seeks to collect and study evidence to determine if the fire started accidentally or was deliberately set (arson).

forensic anthropology: The scientific study of human remains to provide facts for use in court, other legal proceedings, or a civil proceeding.

forensic botany: The scientific study of plants to provide facts for use in a court of law, other legal proceedings, or a civil proceeding.

forensic chemistry: The scientific study of physical evidence and samples to help solve crimes and obtain knowledge for other purposes.

forensic document examination: The scientific authentication (the process of verifying if something is real or true) of signatures and handwriting, as well as the analysis of writing instruments, writing mediums, and office machine products.

forensic engineering: The investigation of malfunctions—or complete failures—in the operation of airplanes, bridges, and other objects and structures.

forensic entomology: The scientific study of insect evidence.

forensic laboratory: A scientific facility where evidence is identified and studied.

forensic nursing: Medical care of victims of violent or abusive acts, and the collection of evidence that can be used in a court of law to catch and prosecute those who have committed these acts.

forensic odontology: The application of dental science to legal investigations; also known as **forensic dentistry**.

forensic pathology: The scientific study of people who died suddenly, unexpectedly, or violently.

forensic science: The process of using science to obtain facts that can be used in court or in other situations where the truth needs to be established.

forensic tool mark identification: The use of scientific methods to match tools—such as screwdrivers and crowbars—to the marks they make when used on objects (often to link a person who is suspected of a crime to the crime); firearms identification is often considered a subspecialty in this field.

forensic toxicology: The study of the effects of chemicals on living organisms for use in court and civil proceedings.

formal witness statement: A witness statement that is made under oath.

friction ridge pattern: A raised fingerprint (loop, whorl, and arch) that appears on the pads of the fingers and thumbs, as well as on the palms, toes, and feet.

grid search: A strategy used at a crime scene or other area that needs to be searched in which the scene is segmented into smaller areas, each of which is searched for evidence.

homicide: Murder.

impression evidence: Anything—such as a tire track, footprint, or tool mark—that leaves an impression at a crime scene or on an object at the scene.

latent fingerprints: Those that are invisible to the human eye.

Locard's exchange principle: The theory that every individual who enters or leaves an area deposits or removes physical material from the scene; developed by Dr. Edmond Locard, a French criminologist.

loop: A type of friction ridge pattern that appears on the pads of the fingers and thumbs, as well as on the palms, toes, and feet. Loop patterns, which recurve back on themselves to form a loop shape, make up about 60 percent of all pattern types.

mass spectrometer: Laboratory technology that is used to conduct chemical analyses on hair, soil, carpet fibers, pollen, and other substances that are collected at a crime scene, or other places where evidence is gathered.

patent fingerprints: Those that are visible to the human eye.

perjury: Lying under oath.

postmortem: The time since death.

rigor mortis: A process after death in which the muscles in the body stiffen (as a result of chemical changes in the muscle structure), resulting in rigidity of the body.

scientific method: A process of experimentation that tests a hypothesis (educated guess).

serology: The study of blood serum.

ten-prints: The fingerprints from all ten fingers.

testify: To provide evidence as a witness in a court of law.

testimony: Evidence that is provided by a competent witness (such as a forensic scientist) under oath in order to establish a fact or facts. Those who lie under oath commit perjury and could be punished.

toxicology: The study of the adverse (negative) effects of chemicals on living organisms.

trace evidence: Physical evidence that results from the transfer of small amounts of materials such as hair, gunshot residue, textile fibers, glass fragments, or paint chips.

trauma: An injury.

whorl: A type of friction ridge pattern that appears on the pads of the fingers and thumbs, as well as on the palms, toes, and feet. Whorl patterns, which form circular or spiral patterns (and look like tiny whirlpools), make up about 35 percent of all pattern types.

witness statement: A written summary of the oral evidence that a witness will give at trial. The statement may be used in place of actual court testimony by the witness, or as a guide to what they will say.

WORDS TO UNDERSTAND

consultant: an experienced professional who is self-employed and provides expertise about a particular subject

cover letter: a one-page letter that details one's interest in a job and their qualifications in an industry specialty (information technology, health care, etc.)

resume: a formal summary of one's educational and work experience that is submitted to a potential employer

Chapter 3

PREPARING FOR THE FIELD AND MAKING A LIVING

EDUCATIONAL PATHS

To become a forensic scientist, you'll need to earn at least a bachelor's degree, but ideally a graduate degree, from a college or university. Other scientists enter the field after receiving training in the military. Some people participate in apprenticeship programs to prepare for technician and other lower-level forensic science jobs. The following sections provide more information on educational paths.

HIGH SCHOOL CLASSES

Many high schools now offer classes or programs in forensic science. If your high school offers these opportunities, be sure to participate in them. Here are some examples of the units of study in a typical forensic science program.

Interns at a laboratory conduct tests and record their findings.

- Observation, Crime Scene Investigation, and Lab Techniques
- Drug Identification and Toxicology
- Death: Meaning, Manner, Mechanism, Cause, and Time
- Handwriting, Forgery, and Counterfeiting
- Forensic Anthropology and Entomology
- Arson/Fire Investigation and Explosions
- Trace Evidence (Hair/Fiber, Pollen/Soil, Glass, Casts)
- Blood and Blood Splatter
- Fingerprints
- Tool Marks and Ballistics
- DNA Fingerprints
- Psychological Profiling and Interrogations/Confessions

In addition to forensic science classes, take as many science courses as possible, including those in biology, chemistry, environmental science, geology, meteorology, and physics.

Other high school classes that will help you to prepare for a career in forensic science include:

- computer science
- mathematics
- English
- speech
- foreign languages
- business, marketing, and accounting classes (if you plan to start your own company)

Some high schools have forensic science clubs, and many have science, computer, and criminal justice clubs. Join these clubs to develop your skills, meet people with similar interests, learn about potential career paths, and, most importantly, have some fun. Join the debate team to help build your public speaking skills and confidence.

Learn about Humber College's Protection, Security and Investigation: Crime Scene Investigation program

COLLEGES AND UNIVERSITIES

You'll need at least a bachelor's degree in forensic science or a degree in biology, chemistry, physics, engineering, etc. (with extensive coursework in forensic science) to work in the field. In a general forensic science program, you'll begin by taking introductory science classes such as general biology, genetics, biochemistry, general chemistry, organic chemistry, physics, and physical biochemistry. Then you'll take the following specialized courses:

- Introduction to Forensic Science
- Forensic Science Ethics and Professional Practice
- Quantitative Analysis
- Human Osteology
- Pattern Evidence
- Forensic Drug Chemistry
- Forensic Toxicology
- Forensic Biology
- Forensic Molecular Biology with Lab
- The Criminal Justice System
- Expert Witness Testimony and Courtroom Demeanor

Some students choose to earn a bachelor's degree in a forensic science specialty. In this case, they take more specialized courses. For example, if you're pursuing a bachelor's degree in forensic engineering, you'll take the following classes:

- Introduction to Forensic Engineering
- Product Liability
- Forensic Engineering Project
- Advanced Forensic Engineering Techniques
- Computer Applications in Forensic Engineering
- Ethics
- Engineering Mathematics

Some government agencies and companies require forensic scientists to have graduate degrees or medical degrees. For example, forensic pathologists must have a medical or dental degree. A master's degree is typically required for managerial positions in laboratories. Lab directors, as well as those in college forensic research positions, need a doctorate. On the other hand, there are no college programs that prepare students for careers as questioned document examiners. They prepare for the field by completing at least two years of training from an experienced examiner. Many examiners receive their training from crime laboratories.

Many forensic scientists work as part-time **consultants** while working full time as college professors. Most college professors have a doctorate degree in their area of expertise. A student earns a doctorate after first earning a bachelor's and master's degree. To earn a doctorate, students must conduct original research, prepare a dissertation (a type of long report), and defend their dissertation before a committee of professors.

Since the educational requirements for each career vary, it's a good idea to investigate educational requirements before you graduate from high school.

INTERNSHIPS

College students typically complete at least one internship as part of their training. An internship is a paid or unpaid learning opportunity in which a student works at a government agency, business, or other organization to get experience. Internships can last anywhere from a few weeks to a year.

OTHER TRAINING

To enter lower-level positions in forensic science (such as crime scene investigator and laboratory analyst), students earn associates and bachelors degrees, participate in apprenticeships, and receive training via the military. Many crime scene investigators who work for police departments are sworn police officers. This means that they have graduated from the police academy as well as completed coursework and/or earned a degree in forensic science or crime scene investigation.

A DAY IN THE LIFE: FORENSIC ANTHROPOLOGIST

I work as a forensic anthropologist at a state government laboratory. Our lab conducts tests on human remains that have been recovered from murder scenes, natural disasters, and plane crashes and other accidents. Of course, we collect and analyze other evidence such as hair, blood, gunshot residue, textile fibers, glass fragments, and paint chips.

I have to admit it: When I was a forensic science student, I was really grossed out by the sight and smell of a corpse. I almost left the field, but I got used to it. Now I respectfully view a corpse as just another piece of evidence that we can study to catch the bad guys. Still, you need a strong stomach to work in this field. Human remains are recovered in all conditions. We might get just a part of a femur, a decomposing body, or a complete skeleton. A skeleton may have soft tissue (muscles, tendons, ligaments, blood vessels, etc.) still attached that will need to be removed so that we can conduct our investigation. We remove this flesh manually by using warm water and detergent, or even with the help of flesh-eating dermestid beetles. This may sound disgusting, but this is what we need to do to begin our investigation.

I spend a lot of time in the laboratory, but I also provide expert witness testimony in court. Because of this role, I'm very careful to prepare detailed reports that establish the chain of evidence and explain my findings. Some of my coworkers get stressed out when they're called to testify, but it doesn't bother me. My job is to present the facts to the judge, jurors, and lawyers on both sides. I explain complicated medical terminology in easy-to-understand terms. My job is not to give an opinion about the guilt or innocence of the defendant.

I love this career because it is all about finding the truth based on hard science. I feel good when the evidence I've analyzed is used to convict a person who has committed a horrible crime, or to help free someone who has been wrongly accused.

MILITARY

You can also receive forensic science training in the military. *Criminal investigators* and *special agents* investigate crimes that have been committed on military property or that involve military personnel. They also perform typical police duties such as guarding military bases and inmates in military correctional facilities, controlling traffic, preventing crime, and responding to crimes or emergencies.

Four U.S. military branches (Air Force, Army, Coast Guard, Navy), as well as many militaries in other countries, provide training for scientists. If you enlist in the U.S. Army, you might have the chance to receive training to work in the Army's Criminal Investigation Command, which is the U.S. Department of Defense's premier investigative agency. If you're selected to become a special agent, you'll complete sixteen weeks of specialized training at the U.S.

Army Military Police School at Fort Leonard Wood, Missouri. Your training will cover everything from crime scene processing to interviews and interrogations.

The military also offers training paths in chemistry, biology, computer science, and other areas that can be a starting point for entering forensic science. Visit TodaysMilitary.com to learn more about potential training paths.

There are a couple of things you should remember before heading to your enlistment office to join the military. First, the military does not employ a large number of criminal investigators and special agents, so it will be difficult to get into these specialties. Second, the military makes every effort to match you with the military career that you desire, but you don't always get a choice. You may want to become a scientist or investigator, but the military may decide you're a better fit as a cook, mechanic, or front-line soldier.

EMPLOYERS OF FORENSIC SCIENTISTS

- Crime laboratories
- Medical examiners' offices
- Police departments and other law enforcement agencies
- Criminal defense firms
- Prosecution attorneys' offices
- Hospital and clinical chemistry laboratories
- Pharmaceutical companies
- Colleges and universities
- Government agencies
- Military

GETTING A JOB

Because you're still in school, it's not yet time to get a job as a forensic scientist. But it never hurts to learn how the job-search process works. There are five general steps in the job-search process that can also be used to apply for an internship.

First, find a job that interests you. Second, submit your **cover letter** and **resume**. The third step is to participate in a phone, online, and/or in-person interview. Once you receive a job offer (the fourth step), you will need to accept or decline the offer (step five).

At this point, learning how to find your first job (or internship) is the most important skill that you can develop. Here are some popular job-search methods for job hunters.

USE YOUR NETWORK

Studies show that more than 50 percent of jobs are filled via networking. "In its simplest form, networking involves having a 'career conversation' with someone for the purpose of exploring careers or job searching to help you answer important career-related questions," according to the University of California at Berkeley Career Center.

During the course of your career, you will have two networks: a personal network and a professional network. You already have a personal network—your family, friends, and classmates. You use it to find out answers to all types of questions, such as: What was the math homework assignment for the class I missed? When do baseball tryouts start? Who is going to the video game competition? Your personal network gives you a lot of good information, but it may also eventually help you land your first after-school job.

Once you get to college, you'll also become part of a professional network that includes your professors, coaches, classmates, bosses, internship directors, and people whom you meet online, including on social networking sites such as LinkedIn.

Don't feel overwhelmed by the concept of networking. First, you're already networking with your friends. Second, you have years to build your skills before you really have to network. And finally, networking just involves talking with people, making new friends, exchanging information, and helping others when they need assistance. If you can talk to people, you can network.

CHECK OUT JOB BOARDS

Many people use internet job boards to apply for and land internships and jobs. They're offered by government agencies, businesses, professional associations, and other organizations. While you're not ready to apply for a job, it's a good idea to check out some job listings to see what types of education and skills are in demand. Here are a few forensic science job boards:

- https://webdata.aafs.org/public/jobs/postings.aspx
- www.crime-scene-investigator.net/employment.html
- www.ascld.org/jobs2

The following job sites offer forensic science job listings:

- www.indeed.com
- www.dice.com
- www.usajobs.gov (U.S. government job board)
- www.jobbank.gc.ca (Canadian government job board)
- www.gov.uk/jobsearch (United Kingdom government job board)

JOIN AND USE THE RESOURCES OF PROFESSIONAL ASSOCIATIONS

A professional association is an organization that is founded by a group of people who have the same career (engineers, biologists, anthropologists, etc.) or who work in the same industry specialty (forensic science, criminal justice, etc.). They offer all types of useful resources for forensic science students and professionals, such as career information, training opportunities, job listings, networking events, and certification. If you want to explore a particular forensic science career or if you're ready to look for a job, association websites should be some of your first stops. One excellent organization is the American Academy of Forensic Sciences (www.aafs.org). It offers membership for college students and forensic science professionals, lists of colleges and universities that offer forensic science degree programs, and resources that will help you to learn more about careers in the field, including the Young Forensic Scientists Forum and the So You Want to Be a Forensic Scientist! e-guide.

Here are some major professional associations for forensic scientists around the world:

- Australian and New Zealand Forensic Science Society, www.anzfss.org
- Canadian Society of Forensic Science, www.csfs.ca
- Chartered Society of Forensic Sciences, www.csofs.org
- International Association for Identification, www.theiai.org
- International Crime Scene Investigators Association, www.icsia.org
- International Society for Forensic Genetics, www.isfg.org

SALARIES FOR FORENSIC SCIENCE TECHNICIANS BY U.S. STATE

Earnings for forensic science technicians vary by state based on demand and other factors. Here are the five states where employers pay the highest average salary and the states in which employers pay the lowest salaries.

Highest Average Salaries:

1. California: $82,650
2. Illinois: $79,630
3. Nevada: $76,160
4. Massachusetts: $75,570
5. Connecticut: $74,560

Lowest Average Salaries:

1. Arkansas: $39,830
2. New Mexico: $40,480
3. North Dakota: $42,240
4. Kentucky: $44,090
5. Maine: $46,930

Source: U.S. Department of Labor

Salaries are highest for forensic scientists who have a lot of experience and expertise.

HOW MUCH CAN I EARN?

Earnings for forensic scientists and other forensic science professionals vary by job title, educational background, the worker's experience level, whether they work full or part time, and other factors. For example, a forensic anthropologist with five years of experience will make more money than someone who is just starting out in their first job after college. A forensic engineer who works for a government agency will typically make less money than one who works for a large private company. Managers usually earn higher salaries than the people they supervise.

PayScale.com reports that full-time forensic scientists earn average salaries of $53,007. The lowest-paid workers earn $36,715, while the highest-paid scientists earn $90,349.

PayScale.com provides the following salary ranges for forensic scientists by specialty:

- crime scene investigator: $30,586 to $73,734
- digital forensics scientist: $43,527 to $115,500
- forensic chemist: $36,828 to $77,652
- forensic engineer: $57,512 to $119,935
- forensic toxicologist: $33,680 to $93,033

It's important to remember that many forensic scientists work on a part-time basis for police departments and other law enforcement agencies while working full time as college professors—often in their specialty (biology, anthropology, or engineering). Here are some salary ranges for college professors by specialty, according to the U.S. Department of Labor:

- anthropology and archaeology: $44,690 to $160,390+
- biological science: $43,160 to $162,470+

- chemistry: $43,110 to $157,130+
- criminal justice and law enforcement: $36,150 to $110,020+
- engineering: $50,280 to $183,590+

The median annual salary for forensic science technicians is $57,850, according to the U.S. Department of Labor. The lowest-paid professionals earn less than $33,880 per year, and the highest earners make $95,600 or more per year.

Forensic chemists in the United States earn salaries that range from $36,828 to $77,652, according to PayScale.com.

Forensic scientists who work full time (thirty-five to forty hours a week) for government agencies, companies, and other organizations often receive fringe benefits such as health insurance, paid vacation and sick days, and other perks. Self-employed workers—those who work for themselves rather than for an employer—do not receive these benefits.

TEXT-DEPENDENT QUESTIONS:

1. What are some typical high school classes for those who want to become a forensic scientist?
2. What are the benefits of joining forensic science associations?
3. How much can forensic scientists earn?

RESEARCH PROJECT:

Visit the websites of college forensic science programs to learn more about different educational options. Find areas that you are interested in, and conduct research to learn more. Email professors in these programs to see if they will talk to you about their program and career paths. This is a great way to build your knowledge—and also your network.

WORDS TO UNDERSTAND

jury: a group of citizens who are selected by lawyers and a judge to participate in a legal proceeding; the jury decides if a defendant (the person accused of a crime) is guilty or innocent

mentor: an experienced professional who provides advice to a student or inexperienced worker (mentee) regarding personal and career development

nonprofit organization: a group that uses any profits it generates to advance its stated goals (protecting the environment, helping the homeless, etc.); it is not a corporation or other for-profit business

simulation: the imitation of a situation or process

Chapter 4

KEY SKILLS AND METHODS OF EXPLORATION

SKILL BUILDING LEADS TO SUCCESS

Scientific and computer skills are extremely important for success as a forensic scientist, but you'll need many other skills, such as soft skills, to perform well in these careers. Soft skills are personal abilities that people need to develop to be successful on the job—communication, work ethic, teamwork, decision-making, positivity, time management, flexibility, problem-solving, critical thinking, conflict resolution, and other skills and abilities. Here are some key traits for forensic scientists.

TEAMWORK AND INTERPERSONAL SKILLS

It takes a team of skilled professionals to solve a crime or identify the cause of an accident. As a forensic scientist, you'll work closely with other scientists, technicians, lawyers, law enforcement professionals, and others. Important traits include strong communication and listening skills, the ability to discuss

Forensic scientists must be able to work well as a member of a team in order to quickly and effectively collect evidence.

your ideas and the ideas of others in a respectful manner, and the ability to follow instructions.

PHYSICAL STRENGTH AND ENDURANCE

If you work at a crime or accident scene, you'll frequently reach, stretch, and crouch as you gather evidence. You may have to carry heavy equipment to and from the crime or accident scene. Some crime scenes are located on challenging terrain. You may have to climb a steep hill to get to the site of an airplane crash, work your way through tight spaces in a cave, or wade into the water to recover a body that was dumped in a pond.

MENTAL AND EMOTIONAL STRENGTH

There is no ignoring the fact that this work can be grisly and depressing. Crime and accident scenes can be very disturbing. Survivors' stories of violence, physical abuse, pain, and suffering are emotionally troubling. Forensic scientists and technicians need to work hard to not let the dark aspects of the job affect their ability to effectively gather and analyze evidence. The fact that their work helps solve crimes and bring closure to the families of murder or accident victims helps many forensic science professionals as they do their jobs.

EXCELLENT COMMUNICATION SKILLS

Forensic scientists and technicians need strong writing skills because they must write detailed reports that summarize their findings. They need top-notch oral communication skills in order to work effectively with members of their team but, most importantly, to testify about their findings in court under oath. They

Forensic scientists must be able to explain complex scientific procedures in language that is easily understandable to juries and other non-scientists.

must be able to explain complex scientific procedures in language that is easily understandable to non-scientists (judges, members of the **jury**, lawyers, the public). They also must remain calm under pressure because their ideas will be challenged by opposing lawyers during cross-examination.

TIME MANAGEMENT

Scientists and technicians must be able to work quickly while still following rules and protocols that seek to protect evidence from contamination and ensure a viable chain of evidence. They may sometimes feel pressured by law enforcement officials and politicians to complete their work quickly. While it's important that they manage their time effectively, scientists and technicians should never work so quickly that the quality of their work is affected.

Forensic scientists need a detail-oriented personality because they are tasked with collecting and managing various types of evidence at crime scenes.

BUSINESS SKILLS

If you plan to launch a consulting business, you'll quickly need to become an expert in basic accounting, marketing, social media, staff management, and the performance of other tasks that keep your company running smoothly.

ADDITIONAL SKILLS

Other important traits of successful forensic scientists and technicians include problem-solving and analytical skills, patience and tenacity, scientific objectivity, ethics and personal integrity, intellectual curiosity, and leadership ability.

EXPLORING FORENSIC SCIENCE AS A STUDENT

There are many ways to learn more about forensic science and careers in the field. Here are some popular methods of exploration.

DO EXPERIMENTS AND OTHER FORENSIC SCIENCE ACTIVITIES

Forensic science is one field where you don't have to wait until you're an adult to get experience. No, you won't be collecting blood samples at a crime scene, but you can conduct experiments and do other activities that will help you to better understand the field. Here are some suggestions.

Try basic chemistry experiments. Ask your science teacher or visit YouTube for some basic experiments. You can also check out the *Illustrated Guide to Home Forensic Science Experiments: All Lab, No Lecture*.

Study a crime scene. Ok, not a real one, but you can choose a room in your house that can serve as a "crime scene." Collect trace evidence such as hair, paint chips, and clothing fibers. Examine hair under a microscope. Dust for fingerprints. Look for footprints or scuffs. Make sketches of the scene, and record all the "clues" you find in a notebook.

Try out a variety of interactive activities at CSI: The Experience—Web Adventures, http://forensics.rice.edu/en/For-Educators/Online-Activities.html.

VOLUNTEER

You probably won't be able to volunteer at a crime lab, but some forensic science associations need help around the office or have formal career exploration programs. For example, students ages fourteen through eighteen can volunteer with the Association of Women in Forensic Science to gain an understanding of forensic science and get help in preparing for college. According to the association's website, volunteers will learn the truth behind some common myths about forensic science; work with a **mentor**, who will provide advice on preparing for college and forensic science careers; participate in community service activities; and get access to science, engineering,

Learn how to dust for fingerprints

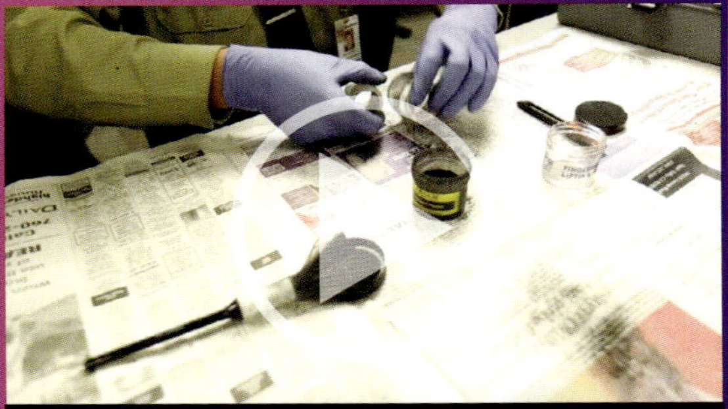

Conducting chemistry experiments in high school is an excellent way to develop your investigative skills.

technology, and mathematics resources. Contact forensic science associations and organizations in your area to learn what type of opportunities are available.

VISIT A MUSEUM

Many science museums have exhibits or workshops that focus on forensic science, or general chemistry or biology. Check out these and other science museums to learn more:

- Museum of Science and Industry, Chicago, www.msichicago.org
- The Franklin Institute, www.fi.edu
- Alcatraz East Crime Museum, www.alcatrazeast.com
- Buffalo Museum of Science, www.sciencebuff.org

Some museums offer programs that allow groups of students to explore forensic science. These usually require a small fee. For example, the Spy Museum

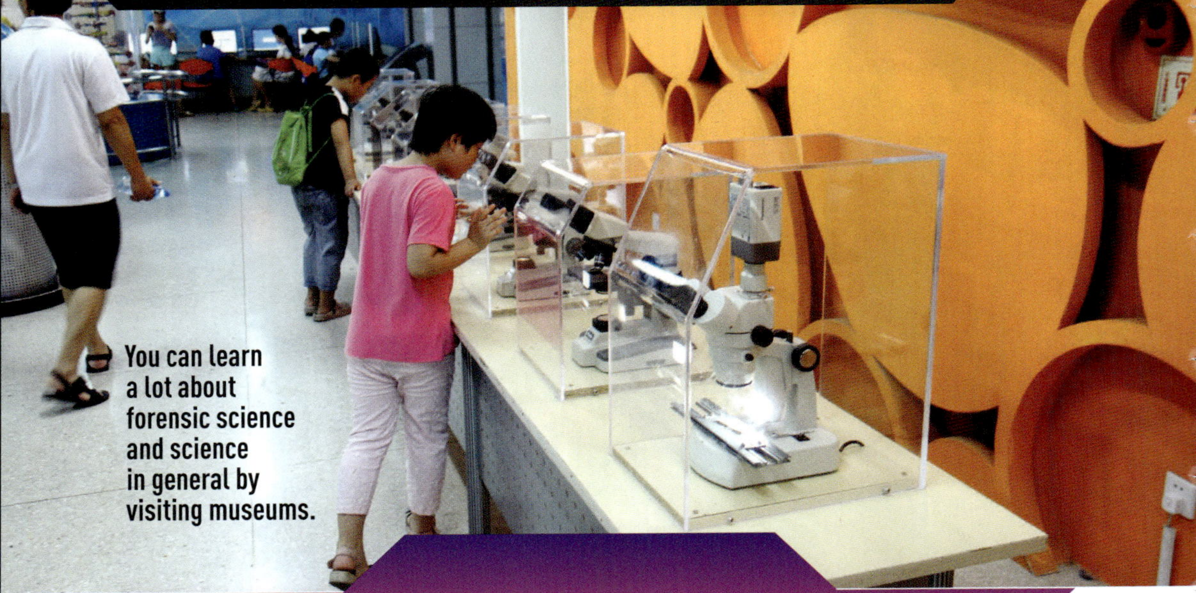

You can learn a lot about forensic science and science in general by visiting museums.

in Washington, D.C., offers the one-day Forensics of Espionage program to students in grade seven and up. Using real FBI forensic equipment and tools, participants study evidence and use the scientific method to attempt to determine the identity of a double agent. The Arizona Science Center in Phoenix offers Teen Science Scene, a one-day program in which participants explore ballistic patterns, footwear evidence, blood splatter, ink and handwriting inspection, fingerprint analysis, and fiber evidence. If you don't live near these museums, contact museums in your area to learn what types of opportunities are available.

VISIT A FORENSIC SCIENCE WEBSITE

There are many informational and interactive websites that will help you explore forensic science and even try to solve an imaginary crime. Check out the following resources for some information and fun.

- Virtual Exhibit on Forensic Science, www.virtualmuseum.ca/sgc-cms/expositions-exhibitions/detective-investigator
- Simon Fraser University Museum of Archaeology & Ethnology—Investigating Forensics, www.sfu.museum/forensics
- CSI: The Experience—Web Adventures, http://forensics.rice.edu
- NOVA—Investigations, www.pbs.org/wgbh/nova/hotscience/int_inve.html

A DAY IN THE LIFE: AVIATION FORENSIC ENGINEER

I work as an aviation forensic engineer for a forensic engineering firm that provides consulting services to aerospace manufacturing companies and government agencies that investigate aviation-related safety issues. I have a bachelor's degree in aeronautical engineering and a master's degree in forensic engineering. I've been an engineer for fifteen years, five of which have been spent in the specialty of forensics engineering. Aviation has always fascinated me. I used to build my own model airplanes when I was a child, and when I was sixteen, I earned my student pilot license. Getting into aviation forensic engineering seemed like a natural progression in my lifelong interest in airplanes, spaceships, satellites, and almost anything else that flies in the sky.

I work on everything from investigating why a single part on an airplane malfunctioned to crash investigations, in which I assess a variety of possible explanations (wear and tear on parts, faultily constructed or repaired parts and systems, human error, terrorist attack, etc.) as to why the plane crashed.

Every day is different. One day, I might receive a portion of a wheel of a 747 for analysis. The next day, I'll be studying a plane's electrical or fuel system.

Let me take you through one recent incident—a fire that occurred on a jetliner as it was about to land. White smoke filled the cockpit as the plane taxied to a stop, and the passengers had to make an emergency exit. Luckily, everyone survived and the fire was put out. It could have been much, much worse.

When we arrived at the scene, we mapped the area, took photographs, and interviewed the flight crew, passengers, ground crew, and bystanders. If the point of origin for the fire is unknown, we examine the plane and its systems to narrow down the causes. We'll look at everything from possible electrical malfunctions and lightning strikes to fuel transmission lines and sprinkler system operations to human error or sabotage. We conduct chemical analysis of samples to detect the presence of accelerants, explosives, and ignition agents, and test materials for flame spread and toxic fumes. We talk to everybody. We look at everything.

Because of the white smoke, the pilots believed that the cause of the smoke was an electrical fire. But our investigation revealed that a fuel fire had started in the engine compartment, which had begun to melt the ducts that supplied heated air to the cabin—hence the smoke.

This is just one example of the type of challenge that we face every day on the job. I really enjoy this job because I like to solve mysteries and because my work has a direct effect on the health and safety of passengers. I like coming to work each day knowing that what I do makes a difference in the world.

Aviation forensic engineers spend hours, and even days, on site to determine what caused a plane crash.

ATTEND A SUMMER CAMP

Another excellent way to investigate forensic science and build your skills is to participate in a summer camp. These camps are offered by forensic science associations, government agencies, colleges, high schools, community groups, companies, and other organizations. One such opportunity is available from the National Student Leadership Conference. It offers a summer Forensic Science program (www.nslcleaders.org/youth-leadership-programs/forensic-science) for high school students. The week-long program is held five times each summer in Washington, D.C. If you participate in this program, you'll get the chance to solve a murder by gathering evidence at a crime scene **simulation**. You'll attend forensic workshops where you'll learn about fingerprint identification, DNA analysis, and other investigative techniques. And you'll get a chance to talk with medical, law enforcement, and legal professionals who will help you learn more about careers in forensic science.

Watch what happens during a forensic science summer camp

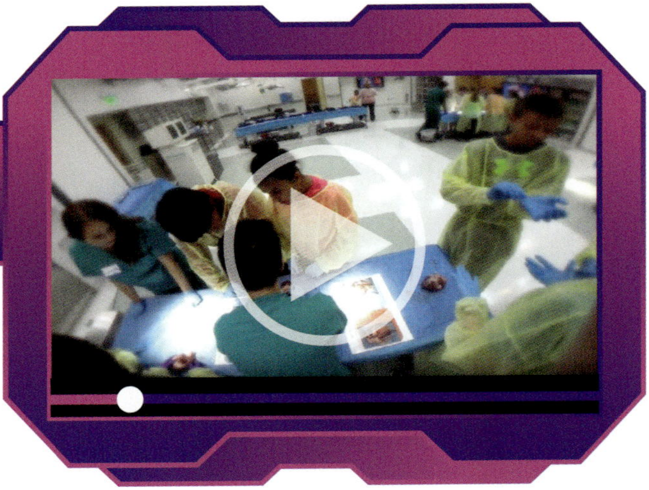

You could also attend a camp that focuses on chemistry, biology, computers, engineering, or anthropology to obtain an introduction to science and technology.

Your high school counselor or science teacher can direct you toward camps in your area, or you can find opportunities by doing a keyword search on the internet. Here are several examples of well-known camps in the United States. Camps are also available in other countries.

- Blueprint Summer Programs—Forensic Science Programs, www.bpsummerprograms.com/forensic-science-pre-college-summer-programs
- Boston Leadership Institute—Forensics Program, http://bostonleadershipinstitute.com/forensics.html
- Georgetown University Forensic Science Academy, https://summer.georgetown.edu/programs/SHS13/forensic-science-institute
- West Virginia University Forensic Science Camp, https://forensics.wvu.edu/students/undergraduate-students/forensic-summer-camp

- Summer Discovery—Crime Scene Investigation Program, www.summerdiscovery.com/crime-scene-investigation

FINDING MORE CAMPS

Many other colleges, organizations, and businesses offer summer forensic science and general chemistry, biology, and computer science camps. Contact schools and organizations in your area to learn more.

JOIN THE TECHNOLOGY STUDENT ASSOCIATION

If you're a middle school or high school student and interested in science, technology, engineering, and mathematics, consider joining the Technology Student Association (TSA, www.tsaweb.org). This national **nonprofit organization** offers sixty competitions at its annual conference—including one in forensic science. The TSA also provides opportunities to develop your leadership skills and compete for money for college. Ask your school counselor or science teacher if your school has a TSA chapter, and if not, ask them to start one.

PARTICIPATE IN A COMPETITION

International, national, and regional associations, corporations, schools, and other organizations sponsor forensic science or general science competitions. These contests are a good way to build your skills and meet people who have the same interests. They're also a lot of fun. Check out the following competitions.

TECHNOLOGY STUDENT ASSOCIATION

This organization offers forensic science competitions for middle school students and high school students. In both competitions, participants take a written test of basic forensic science theory to test their knowledge. Those who score well on the test qualify as semifinalists. Semifinalists collect evidence from—and analyze—a mock crime scene. Learn more: http://tsaweb.org/competitions-programs/tsa/high-school-competitions.

HOSA—FUTURE HEALTH PROFESSIONALS

This international student organization promotes career opportunities in the health care industry. It offers a forensic science competition for high school and college students who are members. Learn more: http://www.hosa.org/sites/default/files/18-19%20FS%20Final.pdf.

THE NATIONAL SCIENCE BOWL

This nationwide academic competition for middle and high school students tests their knowledge of biology, chemistry, earth science, physics, energy, and mathematics. The Science Bowl, which is sponsored by the U.S. Department of Energy's Office of Science, is one of the largest science competitions in the United States. Learn more: www.science.energy.gov/wdts/nsb.

SkillsUSA

This is a national membership organization for middle school, high school, and college students who are preparing for careers in technical, trade, and skilled service occupations. It offers a crime scene investigation competition. Contestants must process a "crime scene" by legally searching for, collecting, and removing evidence of the crime. One member of the team will be asked to lift a latent fingerprint from a preselected item of evidence. Contestants then write a report, draw the crime scene sketch, and mark their evidence. There are also competitions in Criminal Justice and Principles of Engineering/Technology.

SkillsUSA works directly with high schools and colleges, so ask your school counselor or teacher if it is an option for you. Learn more: www.skillsusa.org.

SOURCES OF ADDITIONAL EXPLORATION

Contact the following organizations for more information on education and careers in forensic science, certification, and membership:

- American Academy of Forensic Sciences, www.aafs.org
- Australian and New Zealand Forensic Science Society, www.anzfss.org
- Canadian Society of Forensic Science, www.csfs.ca
- Chartered Society of Forensic Sciences, www.csofs.org
- International Association for Identification, www.theiai.org

JOIN THE SCOUTS

The Boy Scouts and Girl Scouts are membership organizations for boys and girls aged roughly five to eighteen (age ranges vary by country and group). These organizations will help you to become a better person and citizen. They also offer many opportunities to learn things that you didn't know before. When you learn something new in Scouts, you usually receive a merit badge or other type of award.

If you are a boy or a girl in the United States, you can join the Boy Scouts of America (www.scouting.org) and earn merit badges in Chemistry and Fingerprinting. Members of the Girl Scouts of the United States of America (www.girlscouts.org) can earn a variety of Investigation merit badges based on their age level.

You don't have to live in the United States to be a scout. In fact, the Boy Scouts were founded in Great Britain more than 100 years ago. Scouting organizations in Great Britain include The Scout Association (https://scouts.org.uk) and British Boy Scouts and British Girl Scouts Association (https://bbsandbgs.org.uk). If you live in Canada, you can join Scouts Canada (www.scouts.ca).

INTERVIEW A FORENSIC SCIENTIST

Participating in an information interview with a forensic scientist or technician will provide you with a deeper understanding of what careers in the field are like, what education and other training you need to complete, the best and worst parts of the job, and answers to almost any other question you can think of to ask the interviewee. Don't worry, an information interview is not a job interview. It's just a conversation students have with a person in a particular job that helps them learn more about a career. Here are some questions to ask during the interview:

- Can you tell me about a day in your life on the job?
- What are the most important personal and professional qualities for people in your career?

Many forensic scientists are happy to discuss their careers with students.

- What do you like best and least about your job?
- Is your job stressful? If so, please explain why.
- What is the future employment outlook for forensic scientists?
- How is technology changing the field?
- How did you prepare for this career?
- What can I do now to prepare for the field?

Ask your mom or dad, or a family friend, if they know of a forensic scientist or technician who would be interested in discussing their career. Additionally, the public relations departments of forensic laboratories and police departments, forensic science associations, and your school counselor or science teacher can also help arrange an information interview.

TEXT-DEPENDENT QUESTIONS:

1. Why is it important for forensic scientists to be detail-oriented?
2. What can you learn at a forensic science summer camp?
3. What is information interviewing?

RESEARCH PROJECT:

Take a clear set of fingerprints by following the instructions at www.connectionsacademy.com/resources/instructographics/fingerprinting or other websites. Identify the three main fingerprint patterns (loops, whorls, arches) by visiting www.forensicsciencesimplified.org/prints/principles.html and learn more about each type.

WORDS TO UNDERSTAND

augmented reality: a computer-generated system that combines a virtual environment with imaginary elements that are introduced to a real environment; examples include Snapchat lenses and the game Pokémon Go

infrastructure: the systems of a city, region, or nation, such as communication, sewage, water, transportation, bridges, dams, and electric

taxes: money paid to governments by individuals and businesses to help offset the cost of government services or to raise funds for new or ongoing public improvement projects

virtual reality: a computer-generated experience that takes place within a simulated environment using headgear or other equipment that shuts out the real world

Chapter 5

THE FUTURE OF FORENSIC SCIENCE AND CAREERS IN THE FIELD

THE BIG PICTURE

Demand for forensic scientists and technicians will continue to be strong during the next decade. There will always be a need for forensic science professionals to help identify crime victims and solve crimes; determine the identities of missing persons; identify the deceased after terrible train, plane, and other types of crashes, as well as natural disasters; and determine why bridges, other **infrastructure**, airplanes, boats, and a variety of products malfunctioned or failed completely. Employment of forensic science technicians and scientists is expected to grow by 17 percent through 2026, according to the U.S. Department of Labor. That's much faster than the average growth for all careers. "State and local governments are expected to hire additional forensic science technicians

Employment opportunities for forensic engineers will be strong because they will always be needed to determine the causes of train and other types of crashes.

to process their high caseloads. Additionally, scientific and technological advances are expected to increase the availability, reliability, and usefulness of objective forensic information used as evidence in trials. Applicants who have a master's degree should have the best opportunities."

CHALLENGES TO EMPLOYMENT GROWTH

Demand for forensic scientists is good, but a few trends could slow employment growth. The popularity of television shows such as *CSI* and *Bones* have inspired many people to pursue careers in forensic science. If too many people enter the field, open positions will be filled and it will be harder to get jobs. But if the number of people in the United States and other countries continues to grow, it's likely that more crimes will occur and the number of crashes, disasters, and other events that require the expertise of forensic scientists and technicians will increase. This suggests that demand will continue for scientists and technicians.

Many forensic scientists and technicians work for government agencies. These agencies receive funding from **taxes** and other sources. If funding is cut for these agencies, there will be fewer job opportunities for scientists and technicians.

Advances in science and technology have helped the field of forensic science to grow in leaps and bounds. Some people worry that new types of technology might automate (done by computers and/or robots) evidence gathering and many forensic science tests and other procedures. While new scientific procedures and technology may eliminate the need for human workers to perform some basic forensic science tasks, they will create many new opportunities as the science and technology expands what can be done with forensic science evidence gathering and analysis. In short, don't expect to see teams of robot scientists and technicians at a crime scene or accident site anytime soon.

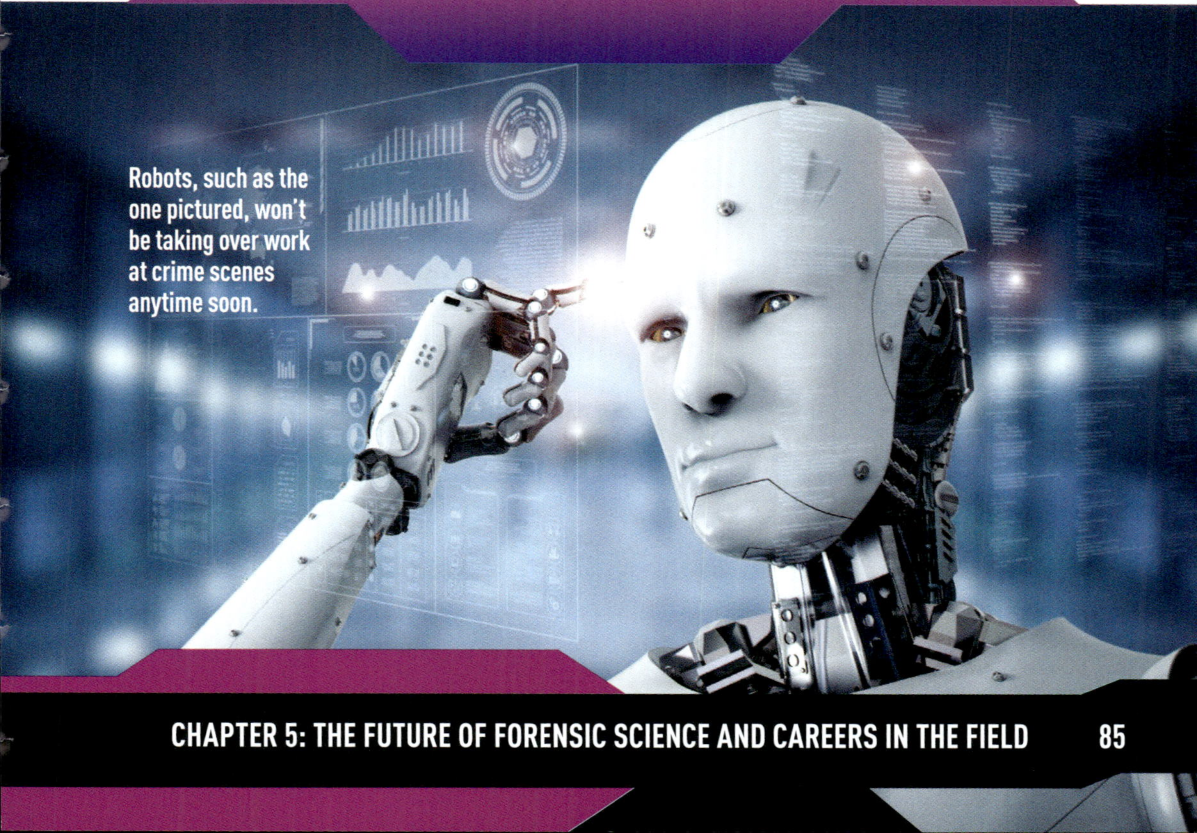

Robots, such as the one pictured, won't be taking over work at crime scenes anytime soon.

WOMEN IN FORENSIC SCIENCE

Men greatly outnumber women in most STEM (science, engineering, technology, mathematics) fields, but did you know that this is not the case in forensic science? A study by the Associated Press found that women comprise 75 percent of graduates of forensic science programs. Why is forensic science so popular with women? A study by researchers at Marshall University found that 30 percent of forensic science students who were surveyed said that they wanted to enter the field because they were inspired by strong female characters on TV crime shows such as *CSI*, *Bones*, and *NCIS*. Another important reason cited was students' love of solving puzzles. Finally, the researchers reported that forensic science students said they wanted to "do something different every day, something that has a direct application on peoples' lives, and can bring justice to a victim," aspects "that are lost in many STEM research laboratories." The Association of Women in Forensic Science (www.awifs.org) is a good resource for young women who are considering a career in forensic science.

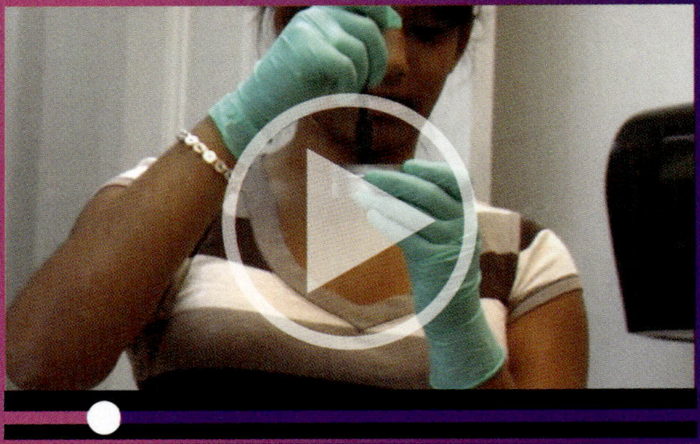

Discover why a large number of women enter the field of forensic science

THE FUTURE OF FORENSIC SCIENCE

Forensic science has come a long way in the past 100 years. For example, fingerprints that were once only able to be detected by dusting can now be spotted by lasers, LED devices, and other high-tech methods. Forensic scientists no longer need to spend hours comparing fingerprints from a crime scene with a stack of prints pulled from a file cabinet. They now use automated fingerprint

Forensic science is a popular option for young women.

New mobile fingerprint scanning systems will allow police to identify a potential suspect in under a minute at a crime scene.

identification systems to quickly match crime scene prints with those of known offenders on file. Finally, *The Independent* reports that police in the United Kingdom are testing a new mobile fingerprint scanning system that allows police to identify a potential suspect in under a minute at the scene of an incident. "From the moment we take the fingerprint we're getting results right through to the Police National Computer check and the photograph in less than a minute," explained Chief Inspector Ian Williams of the West Yorkshire Police.

So what else does the future hold for forensic science? Here are some ways that technology and science will change the field in the future.

- Portable forensic labs will be in wide use at crime and accident scenes, greatly increasing the speed at which evidence is tested.
- Evidence will increasingly be collected from smartphone interaction with entertainment and telematic systems in vehicles. This information can tell investigators when car doors were opened and shut and when the car stopped, as well as provide data about airbags, seat belts, and other vehicle features.
- Virtual autopsies, which are already being conducted, will become increasingly popular because they are noninvasive and do not damage the body or evidence.
- Microbiomes, which the National Institute of Justice defines as "communities of microorganisms that live on or in people, plants, soil, oceans, and the atmosphere," will increasingly be used in forensic science because no two people's microbiomes are the same. They will be used to supplement the use of human DNA for associating people with evidence and environments, and as an indicator of time since death. Additionally, microbiomes that are found in different soils can be used to link a suspect, victim, or evidence to a particular outdoor environment.

- Advanced DNA analysis techniques may lead to the generation of detailed physical descriptions—and computer illustrations—of suspects.
- Forensic scientists will increasingly use **virtual reality** technology to re-create crime scenes for further study, or for use with juries and judges.
- When a forensic scientist or technician is not yet on the scene of a crime or accident, police officers may wear **augmented reality** (AR) headsets or use other AR systems so that forensic scientists who are off-site can instruct them on which evidence to collect.
- Computer algorithms may be created that can identify would-be criminals before they can commit a crime.

IN CONCLUSION

Can you see yourself using the latest cutting-edge scientific techniques and technology to solve crimes or determine why an airplane crashed? Do you enjoy solving problems? Are you looking for a career that offers good pay and great job prospects? If so, then a career as a forensic scientist could be in your future.

I hope that you'll use this book as a starting point to discover even more about careers in forensic science. Talk to forensic scientists and technicians about their careers, use the resources of professional organizations, attend forensic science summer camps, and most importantly, collect some fingerprints, conduct science experiments, and investigate a mock crime scene to build your skills. Good luck on your career exploration!

TEXT-DEPENDENT QUESTIONS:

1. Why is demand growing for forensic scientists?
2. What factors could slow career growth in forensic science?
3. How will the field of forensic science change in the future?

RESEARCH PROJECT:

Spend some time exploring the future of forensic science. How will technology change the work of forensic scientists? Write a report about your findings and present it to your class.

PHOTO CREDITS

6: Nanditha Rao | Dreamstime.com
10: Mast3r | Dreamstime.com
12: Mira Agron | Dreamstime.com
15: Corepics Vof | Dreamstime.com
18: Peter Kim | Dreamstime.com
20: James Menges | Dreamstime.com
23: Esben Hansen | Dreamstime.com
27: Michael J. Ermath | U.S. Food & Drug Administration
30: Anthonyata | Dreamstime.com
33: National Institute of Standards and Technology
36: Lightfieldstudiosprod | Dreamstime.com
38: Drzaribu | Dreamstime.com
40: Imagevillage | Dreamstime.com
42: Forance | Dreamstime.com
44: Michael J. Ermarth | U.S. Food & Drug Administration
48: Flair Images | Dreamstime.com
50: Tetyana Halanchak | Dreamstime.com
60: James Steidl | Dreamstime.com
62: Viacheslav Iacobchuk | Dreamstime.com
64: Lisa F. Young | Dreamstime.com
66: Lisa F. Young | Dreamstime.com
67: Photographerlondon | Dreamstime.com
68: Kreangkrai Indarodom | Dreamstime.com
71: Rakratchada | Dreamstime.com
72: Lovephoto227 | Dreamstime.com
75: Bambi L. Dingman | Dreamstime.com
80: Auremar | Dreamstime.com
82: National Institute of Standards and Technology
84: Vasilis Ververidis | Dreamstime.com
85: Kittipong Jirasukhanont | Dreamstime.com
87: Mark Adams | Dreamstime.com
88: Jf123 | Dreamstime.com

Cover Photo: © pogonic | Shutterstock; © Mega Pixel | Shutterstock

FURTHER READING

Heos, Bridget. *Blood, Bullets, and Bones: The Story of Forensic Science from Sherlock Holmes to DNA*. New York: Balzer + Bray, 2016.

Lyle, Douglas P. *Forensics For Dummies*. 2nd ed. Hoboken, N.J.: For Dummies, 2016.

McDermid, Val. *Forensics: What Bugs, Burns, Prints, DNA, and More Tell Us About Crime*. New York: Grove Press, 2016.

Saferstein, Richard. *Forensic Science: From the Crime Scene to the Crime Lab*. 3rd ed. New York: Pearson, 2015.

Thompson, Robert Bruce, and Barbara Fritchman Thompson. *Illustrated Guide to Home Forensic Science Experiments: All Lab, No Lecture*. San Francisco: Maker Media, Inc., 2012.

INTERNET RESOURCES

www.aafs.org/home-page/students/choosing-a-career: This guide from the American Academy of Forensic Sciences provides information on education and careers in a variety of forensic science areas, including anthropology, digital and multimedia sciences, odontology, toxicology, engineering sciences, pathology/biology, psychiatry and behavioral science, criminalistics, jurisprudence, and questioned document examination.

www.bls.gov/ooh/life-physical-and-social-science/forensic-science-technicians.htm: This section of the *Occupational Outlook Handbook* features information on job duties, educational requirements, salaries, and the employment outlook for forensic science technicians.

www.prospects.ac.uk/job-profiles/forensic-scientist: This website provides information on career paths, job duties, required skills, and earnings for forensic scientists, with a special emphasis on forensic science in the United Kingdom.

https://science.howstuffworks.com/forensic-lab-technique.htm: Visit this website to learn about the history of forensic science and what happens in a forensic lab.

INDEX

INDEX

EDUCATIONAL VIDEO LINKS

[illegible]

[illegible]ional requirements, key skills for success, and careers in forensic science: http://x-qr.net/1DHD

Learn more about the Forensic Chemistry Unit at the Denver Police Crime Lab: http://x-qr.net/1DJz

Chapter 3:

Learn about Humber College's Protection, Security and Investigation: Crime Scene Investigation program: http://x-qr.net/1D8f

Chapter 4:

Learn how to dust for fingerprints: http://x-qr.net/1G7Q

Watch what happens during a forensic science summer camp: http://x-qr.net/1G97

Chapter 5:

Discover why a large number of women enter the field of forensic science: http://x-qr.net/1EzC

AUTHOR BIOGRAPHY

Andrew Morkes has been a writer and editor for more than twenty-five years. He is the author of more than twenty-five books about college-planning and careers, including all of the titles in this series, many titles in the Careers in the Building Trades series, the *Vault Career Guide to Social Media*, and *They Teach That in College!?: A Resource Guide to More Than 100 Interesting College Majors*, which was selected as one of the best books of the year by the library journal *Voice of Youth Advocates*. He is also the author and publisher of "The Morkes Report: College and Career Planning Trends" blog.